I want people laughing,

happy and healthy. That's what this book is about.

When I teach vegetable sculpture and cooking classes, when I cook in my restaurant, and when I lead Wok 'N Walk tours of Philadelphia Chinatown, lots of people ask me, "Joe, why don't you write books?" I love to share stories and recipes with my customers, students and friends. Now I will share with you, too.

I hope my philosophy and special ways of cooking will help you, motivate you, and make you laugh. Within this book, you will find my One Second Sculpture, the quickest food sculpture you will ever see. You will see Five Second Cooking, a recipe that made Ellen DeGeneres laugh like crazy on her show. And I hope my Ten Second Philosophy of Success inspires you to follow your dreams and never give up.

Here is why I thank America. I was born in Hong Kong. When I came to the United States, my English was poor. Even though I could read, I didn't know how to speak the language. I appreciate my American teachers, friends and customers. They've been patient with me. They helped me go to SUNY College at Oneonta as well as Culinary Institute of America, where I majored in nutrition. People taught me English. They gave me the knowledge and skills I needed to survive in this country. In their kindness, they taught me how to care for and love other people. This is an autobiography book. I have been in the United States for 33 years. I have gained skills and philosophies I'd like to give away to you before I pass on. I owe America very much. Everybody can use these life skills to do good for people and society.

This is also a cookbook. I want to share with young people and anyone who loves to learn Asian culinary art, Asian ingredients and Asian culture. Many American chefs and culinary students join my Wok 'N Walk tours of Philadelphia Chinatown. Many are unfamiliar with Asian ingredients. When I show them fresh water chestnuts, for instance, they think it is truffle, or black olive, or a kind of root. Once I explain its functions and how to cook it, they are amazed. Asian ingredients include Chinese, Japanese, Thai and Vietnamese. These ingredients make Asian sauce unique. I will share with you my Asian culinary secrets discovered from forty years of experience.

This is a simple, funny, yet meaningful book. Many chefs have stories about how they succeed and how they struggle with the real world. It is not easy for first-generation immigrants to make it in this country. I will tell you how I have come through difficulties, fighting for dreams. I will tell you of struggle, vegetable sculpture, secret recipes, Asian culture, and how the good hearts of people helped me through.

I hope this book is useful and amusing. Once in a while, when you are down, you can read it again. If I make you laugh, motivate you, and help you not give up your dreams, then I am happy. Thank You, America!

Contents

AUTOBIOGRAPHY

To my parents, Mr. and Mrs. Poon
To my American parents, Mr. and Mrs. Wood
To my school, State University of New York College at Oneonta

My Life Stories: Raising Up from the Dirt!

My name is Joseph K. K. Poon. Joseph is my Christian name. Poon is my last name. In the middle I have two Ks. Kwok, meaning country. And Keung, meaning strong. One more K, people might mistake who I am. After all, I'm not the Ku Klux Klan!

I was born in Hong Kong, where I went to Catholic school during World War II. I grew up in a poor family with nine brothers and sisters. Four sisters passed away from lack of food and medicine. I survived by taking food from garbage cans and begging money at hotels and on the street. Being poor doesn't mean disaster or end of the world. Having to scrounge doesn't mean you cannot raise yourself up from "the dirt." Poverty told me to keep going, keep learning, and keep improving. Poverty said, be strong and never give up. Kind people showed me how. If I can make it, you can too. Here is how.

In 1968, I graduated from Hong Kong La Salle High School.

My American parents, Mr. and Mrs. Wood.

When I was a little kid, I loved playing Ping Pong. Every morning at 7:00, I ran to the playground. School started at 8:00, so I could play the game for an hour. During break and after school, all I did was play Ping Pong. My studies were left behind, especially my English, which was poor. I failed English. My mom was upset. She burned my Ping Pong paddles and forbid me to play the game ever again.

I couldn't give up Ping Pong in my life because I love it so much. I had no more paddles. Instead, I used a pencil box for a paddle. The pencil box was thin and small. I had to use a lot of force and skills to practice. I kept going with the pencil-box paddle. I became a Ping Pong champion at my elementary school and then a champion in SUNY at Oneonta.

Nowadays kids are lucky. Most of them have their parents' love and good education to help them reach their goals.

Even with such good fortune, though, people must work hard to become a champion. It is easier to work hard when you follow what you love. Pencilbox Ping Pong was my first success in life. Because I loved the game.

So remember, when you find something you love, go for it, keep practicing, and never give up.

My best friend in my life, my parents, Mr. and Mrs. ____

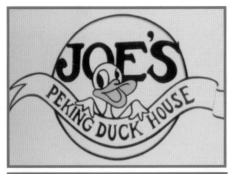

Turn your Loss into Gain

In 1972 I left Hong Kong to travel around the world. Here is why I left my country. When I was 25 years old, I worked in Hong Kong Airport. Back then, you needed some "Chinese connections". If you didn't have someone to sponsor you and pay money, you couldn't get a job. I was lucky. I had a connection to work at the airport. But turns out, I wasn't so lucky after all.

This is a story about how when losing everything, you can gain a lot. I worked hard at the airport and made money. But hard work and money didn't make me successful. Working for this big company required a long time for people to discover your skills. You had to be patient, patient, patient. And to get ahead in this job, you had to kiss butt and bribe people. I couldn't stand it. I am not that type. So I resigned!

I went to England. I met the wrong people there. I connected with a cousin. When I asked for help, she gave me indifference. This felt like disaster for me. But I didn't give up. Eventually, I arrived in Philadelphia. I found a friend who went to school with me when we were eleven years old. He had become a dentist in Chinatown. He helped me. He encouraged me to go to college at Oneonta for higher education. He is my best friend in my life, Dr. Augustine Au. Thanks to my friend and kind Americans, I had a chance to finish school. This is a critical turning point in my life.

This might sound good, but no. My life turned bad again. I lost my first Peking Duck House that I opened in 1979. In 1984, I was a partner with three people for my second restaurant, Joe's Peking Duck House in Chinatown. The restaurant was successful, so we opened another one. Then in 1994, I lost ownership because things did not work out with my partners. In one day, I lost a partnership, two restaurants and six houses. This felt like the end of the world.

You'd think this was all bad, losing more than a million dollars in one day. But, no! Instead, I thank these partners who left me with nothing. They made me stronger and better. After losing everything, I worked four jobs and saved money to open Joseph Poon Asian Fusion Restaurant. This is now successful. I won many awards, have been featured in newspaper stories, appeared on TV, and held many charity events—all this without having to consult partners. I became stronger, better and more sharing.

I may have lost a lot of money, but I gained success and the caring of other people. This is more important than wealth. So remember this in life: When you lose much, pull yourself up with a strong mind and warm heart. In the end, your life will turn around. With all you gain from your loss, you can become successful and happy.

AWWW YEAH

Channel 6, Mark H., 1979

Share What you Know

When I was in Hong Kong at La Salle High School, the teacher asked our class to write a composition that answered the question, "What do you want to be when you grow up?" I wrote that I wanted to be a teacher.

Turns out, I majored in food nutrition then become a chef. And my dream came true: I gave lectures at Buck's County Community College, Nutrition and Hospitality College, and Pennsylvania College of Technology, etc.

When I arrived in Philadelphia on November 9, 1972, my English was poor. I knew a few words such as "Thank you," "I am sorry," and "How do you do." The first English sentence someone said to me that day was "What's up man?" I didn't know what this meant. In my English classes I never heard such words. I kept saying, "I am sorry, I don't understand." I felt scared and lost. I wanted to take the plane back to Hong Kong. I felt like crying, but I had no choice. I grit my teeth. I forced myself to be patient,

work hard, never give up, keep learning and find confidence.

That was then. Now I enjoy teaching. First, I have a big mouth. Second, I love to share all the secrets "stole" from other chefs. And third, love to see students learn new skills. My philosophy is "You love to learn. I love to share."

My cooking skills landed me on th Jay Leno Show. Jackie Chan and Chow Yun-Fat were there, too. Later was master of ceremonies at the Sysc Atlantic City Convention. I felt luck and honored to be invited by the American Culinary Federation to dc demonstration for 300 executive che from around the world. When I finished they stood up with their applause. This almost made me cry. So hard to believe that sharing my skills and knowledge received this

Federation to do a demonstration for 300 executive chefs from around the world. When I finished they stood up with their applause. This almost made me cry. So hard to believe that sharing my skills and knowledge received this respect from these honorable chefs.

When you do what you love, you learn much. Then comes your turn to share. That makes people happy and warms your soul like hot Luoshong soup.

Don't be Afraid to Make Mistakes

You should see my hands. I burned them many times. I learned a big lesson one early Saturday morning in 1985 when a fire accident happened in my restaurant. I roasted pig that day at five o'clock in the morning. It caught fire, burned the whole kitchen, and ruined the restaurant. I burned my face, my hair and my hands. I learned from this experience to be careful. Everyday now, I check the gas and equipment to make sure everything works well. We roast duck everyday, nearly 200 of them sometimes. I carefully check these ducks and roasted pigs to make sure they have been hung the right way in the equipment.

When you make mistakes on your recipe—too spicy or too salty—don't feel bad. As Americans say, "What do you expect? We are human beings; we make mistakes." When we do something wrong, fine. Just try again. Recipes are guidelines, not perfect ways to prepare tasty dishes. When you can't find ingredients from the recipes, you can change them. Use other ingredients to replace them. The sauce is important; a good taste is imperative. But if you are without certain ingredients, you can still make a good recipe.

When I was young and made mistakes, I still had time to learn and correct them. But when you come to a certain age (now I am 56), there is not much time left to make mistakes. But they still happen anyway. Life is short. So be tolerant with people, and be strict with yourself. When people make mistakes, don't insult them or curse them. Give them a chance to correct their slipups. When you make your own mistakes, you can change. Keep improving yourself to become a better person.

Accept your stumbles. Never fear your own blunders. You will find some mistakes turn to discovery. The wrong ingredient might be better than the one intended. This is how life goes.

Ten Second Philosophy of Success

It takes only ten seconds to tell you my philosophy of success: Hard work, experience, wisdom, confidence and capability. However, it has taken a long time, my whole life, to fully understand what these words mean.

First is hard work. When I was in Hong Kong at La Salle High School, one of my teachers told us, "I don't worry if you guys are smart or not. I only worry about lazy people." Lazy people find it hard to succeed. We all know the story called, "Rabbit and Turtle." The rabbit knows he can run faster, so he takes his time. He is lazy and rests along the way. The turtle moves slowly, but he keeps walking until he reaches his destination and wins. In real life, "turtle" people are more likely to win than "rabbit" people. I am not smart. But I work very hard.

Second is experience. Successes are experience, but mistakes are even better experience. From what

Turn your Scars into Stars

This is the story of culture shock and Marijuana Egg Drop soup. In my second year of college at Oneonta, I was majoring in nutrition. Mr. Caswell, my counselor in the foreign student department, posted a note on the bulletin board for me. It said, "Mr. Joseph Poon is a volunteer to cook for you. So please call."

One day there was a gentleman. I remember his name is Jeff. He was a basketball player at my school—a popular fellow. He called me one Sunday and asked me to fix him a dinner to impress his girlfriend. He had a date that night. When I began cooking, he asked, "Joe, could you please put the sauce on the side? That way I can pretend I cooked it myself. I can impress my girlfriend, and maybe I'll get lucky tonight. Ooooh! Hot stuff!"

At that time my English was not so good. And I didn't know much about American culture, including ingredients, so I kept trying to learn. The student gave me $2.50 to buy ingredients. (Back then, a quarter bought a head of lettuce.) But he told me, "Before you buy anything, look in my refrigerator and freezer to see what ingredients you can use." I found some eggs. At this time, my cooking was just okay—not up to high standards. I had learned basic egg drop soup from a restaurant. I used two of those eggs for egg drop soup. Usually you use scallions on top, but I couldn't find any scallions in the refrigerator. In the freezer, though, I found some small, beautiful green leaves. They looked like thyme. I dumped them in the soup, and they mixed innicely. Then I thought I better ask if this was okay. The student was taking a shower. I called into him, "Okay I use your greens from freezer on the soup?" Mama mia, he went crazy. "Noo!" he cried. He ran from the shower you've read so far, you can see I have made plenty of mistakes. I cooked marijuana egg drop soup—big mistake that turned out okay. I burned my restaurant—this taught me to check the gas and equipment every day.

Experiences like this have taught me much in the restaurant business, especially when things go wrong. How can I provide consulting service in cooking skills and restaurant management? How can I create a menu of Lobster Feast in 25 minutes? How can I consider food cost, easy operation for staff in the kitchen and detailed instructions for managers, all the while keeping customers satisfied with our food and service? This I learned through experience.

Third is wisdom. Sometimes I create different recipes based on what people have shown me in America and while traveling. I have learned from different people—everyone from experienced chefs to youngsters, all in different cultures. I am no genius, but these people's stories make me bright. These days, it's much easier to build wisdom. Many of you have wise parents, teachers and coworkers around you. They can share with you their mistakes, which then turn into good advice. You need wisdom to make good decisions. Try to stay humble. Listen to others. Digest what they say. Listening to other people's stories and mistakes makes you wiser and stronger.

Last, but not least, are confidence and capability. They are interrelated forces for your success. If you have no confidence in yourself, you cannot succeed. When you go to an exam, if you doubt you can pass, you will probably fail. When you open a restaurant, if you don't believe you can run it well, no need to bother. If you think you are incapable to make French Demi-Glace, Mexican Mole Chicken, Italian Polenta, Jewish Latke, Chinese Dim Sum and Peking Duck, please rethink your career to be a chef. Confidence in yourself is not easy. It takes hard work, experience and wisdom. It takes time to know who you are. You fight with yourself to win.

Some people say, "Where there's a will, there's a way." Other say, "Some succeed because they are destined to, but most succeed because they are determined to." Either way, you need these five "ingredients": hard work, experience, wisdom, confidence and capability. This is how you succeed.

and flew into the kitchen. It was too late. I had put all his marijuana into the egg drop soup.

This is the first soup I ever made for a student. And it was very tasty. I think they both got high that night, and I don't know what happened. Maybe a little hanky panky. With our different cultures, I didn't know about those leaves. But things turned out well, and the handsome man and his girlfriend were both happy that night. Wow, hot stuff!

Scars can turn to stars. Accept the bad. It can turn to good.

Awesome

哲學人生雕花

This is going to be fun and Awesome !

When I was twenty years old, I worked for an airline catering company (ACL) in Hong Kong. This was my first experience in food service. While there, I was amazed at the chef's carved fruit, vegetable centerpieces and food sculptures. He created beautiful roses from potatoes soaked in cherry juice. When I asked the chef to teach me, he refused.

I didn't give up! I bought a hundred potatoes and taught myself by tracing the form of the rose onto the potato. I practiced nearly an hour a day. At first, I was not good at all! My roses looked wrong. But after three months, I was able to carve a beautiful rose in one and half minutes. Then I went on to practice sculpting all kinds of shapes.

This art is my passion. Now I want to give you the lessons the chef in Hong Kong refused to give me.

Chapter 2

Vegetable Sculpture

Give Your Heart in Different Ways

One Second Sculpture
Hearts Shine Brighter than Diamonds

Love is priceless!

The simplest thing I do in my life is food sculpture. For example, I can finish a sculpture in one second. Here it is: I cut a grape in half and create a heart. That is One Second Sculpture. If you don't have grapes, you can make the heart from kiwi, radish, tomato or cucumber.

Sometimes, you don't need to buy expensive things to make your honey happy. You simply use your mind and heart to create something. A special grape heart costs you only one or two cents. Let's say you make your girlfriend angry and want to apologize. You buy some grapes and make a few hearts. You

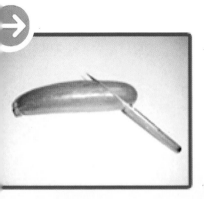  

put them in a diamond box and go home. You say, "Honey, I love you," and give her your grape hearts. She will smile and forgive you, I hope. You need to share your genuine love and spend time with your honey. Otherwise, she will run away. That's why I am still single.

I am a cheap guy. I don't buy flowers or expensive things. All the girls I meet, I use the grape or potato rose to impress them. They laugh, and sometimes they fall in love with me. This is nice for your friends, too. When people are down, try a grape heart, you can make them laugh.

Even if you do not have much money, you can give your caring and love. People will understand what's inside this little grape heart.

Watermelon

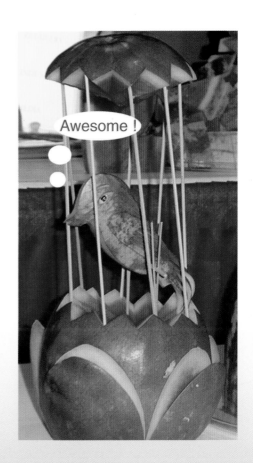

Awesome !

Hello !

Pumpkin Sculpture

The first pumpkin I ever saw was in the United States. I decided to sculpt a bird from the biggest pumpkin I could find. I created this for the School of Fine Arts in SUNY College at Oneonta.

Half-Ton Food Sculpture
Set Yourself Apart from the Rest

This sculpture took me three hours to finish, and it weighed one hundred fifty pounds.

The largest sculpture I've done was from thousand pounds of watermelons. I sculpted a dragon that was one hundred feet long and weighed half a ton. Sunny and Pat, the President and Manager of Philadelphia Regional Produce Market, supplied me with all the watermelons I needed. They also donated more watermelons for my fundraising for children, cancer and the elderly. Thank you, Sunny and Pat.

When you sculpt from fruits or vegetables, create something different from what other people have done. Do something unique and challenging—this is the key to your success as a food sculptor.

Karl Albrecht said, "There are only two ways to establish competitive advantage: do things better than others or do them differently." In today's world, doing things better than other people is difficult. But you can do things differently, which makes you stand out.

求新求變

Keep learning and flexible to change!

CHEF POON

on TONIGHT Show
Jay Leno

CHEF POON

on TONIGHT Show
Jay Leno

Jay Leno

ELVIS

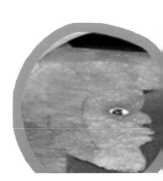

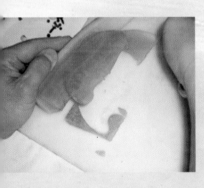

飲 水 思 源

hen drinking water think of its source!

Hello !

Watermelon Sculpture Debut

Remember Those who Helped You

Watermelons are great to carve because, unlike apples or potatoes, you can sculpt a hundred pieces from one watermelon. You can even carve the face of Elvis or Jay Leno. To do so, simply follow the steps shown.

Through kindness of many people, my food sculpture has become known. First of all, the National Watermelon Promotion Board discovered my work. In 1999, Irene Baker became my marketing agent. She is the best partner as well as the best teacher and friend in my life. Working with her is the turning point of my career. She introduced me to a woman named Samantha from Florida, who guided me to many shows and demos. For example, we attended an event with the

Produce Marketing Association. Every year these events attract thousands of people with all kinds of produce from around the world.

In this way, one thing led to another. Doing these demos for four years led to appearances in newspapers, magazines and TV. I appreciate Irene Baker and Samantha. They were the first people to allow me to show my food sculptures to the public. I worked hard for them, and they treated me like family.

This is why I say, when people give you a chance, don't let the opportunity go by. Work hard for them. And never forget the people who helped you. Thank you all, Irene, Samantha, and National Watermelon Promotion Board, from the bottom of my heart!

Two Mice (from Two Radishes)

Using radish, you can make a funny mouse. This is easy. Take a look at the pictures. While you carve the mice, be careful and patient. Remember to take your time, set your goal, set your mind, and don't give up. I know you can do it.

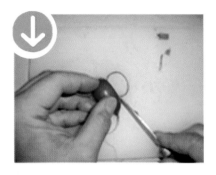

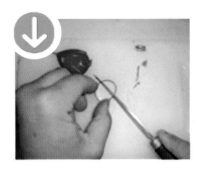

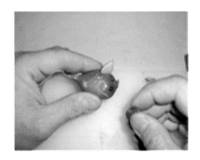

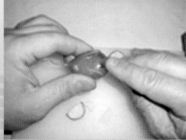

有信心鐵杵成針

If you have confidence, you can grind an iron pestle down to a needle!

Instructions:

1. Cut 1/5 of the radish and make a round piece as the picture shows to make a pair of ears.
2. Put a cut on both sides of the radish to put the ears in.
3. Draw two holes between the two cuts for the eye.
4. Make a V cut at the bottom of the radish.
5. Cut the round piece into half, then scoop the white part and make them thinner to place as ears of the mouse.
6. Put two black pepper corns into two holes to make them like eyes. Then put a white piece of radish into the V cut to make it like "cheese" in its mouth.

Awesome !

A Rose for Your Love

Share your Skill

The rose is the first food sculpture I learned. This is the shape I practiced for three months, after the chef refused to teach me. Now I love to share this skill. What joy to see younger people learn to carve shapes from fruits and vegetables. After you practice creating sculptures from the traces in this book, you can pass the skill on as well. Please show someone else what you learn. Sharing is as beautiful as the rose you carve.

To make the rose, trace from the picture in this book for at least 45 minutes a day. Potatoes are good to practice on. Or you can use carrots, pumpkins, turnips, watermelons, beets or apples. This is a complicated sculpture; so don't feel discouraged if you mess up. When you make a sorry-looking rose, try again.

When your skill improves, use a sculpted rose to express your love. You can give it to your mom for Mother's Day. Or you can pass it to a friend who is feeling down. This rose is a gift from your heart and your mind. You made it with love.

Share with others!

分甘同味

I dedicate this rose beet to one of my best teachers in my life, Dr. Frances H. Gailey! She is in charge of my Joseph Poon Scholarship Foundation in SUNY at Oneonta!

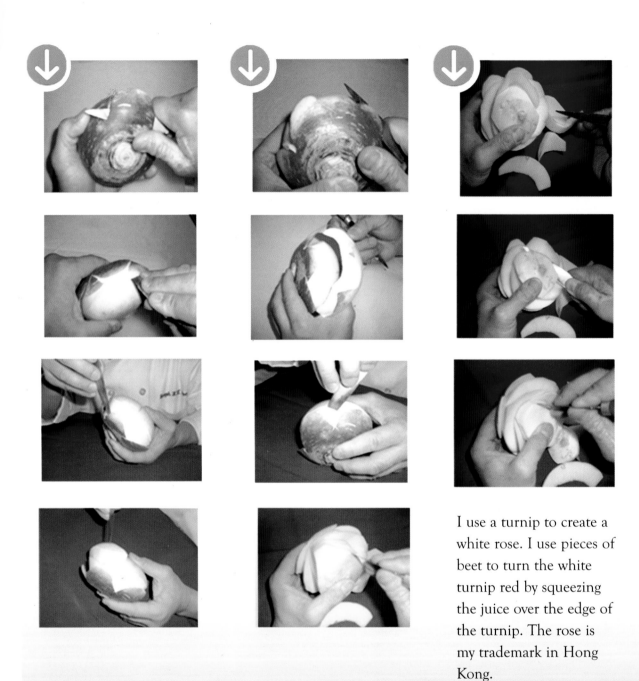

I use a turnip to create a white rose. I use pieces of beet to turn the white turnip red by squeezing the juice over the edge of the turnip. The rose is my trademark in Hong Kong.

手得雲開見夕明

Rose is red, Life is not always blue!
There is always a silver line in the cloud!

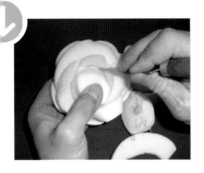

I cut a beet. I need "beet-le juice"! You need another four years to improve yourself...

Just as the "beet-le juice" turns you a better person in the world.

Be Optimistic!
C-CAP Students!
Have a Higher Education!

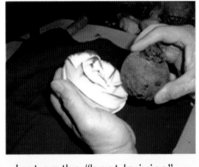

This is the beginning of your high school. After four years, you'll graduate and become a beautiful rose. But not yet...

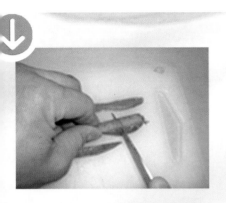

Yellow Bird

Bring Peace to the World !

Instructions:

1. Slice both sides of the yellow squash to make wings.

2. Make two triangle pieces of carrot to hold wings.

3. Cut a piece of carrot to make the beak.

4. Use tooth pick to make two holes and put two black pepper corns to make eyes.

5. Insert the beak into the yellow squash and done.

Peep ! Peep !

Joseph K. on

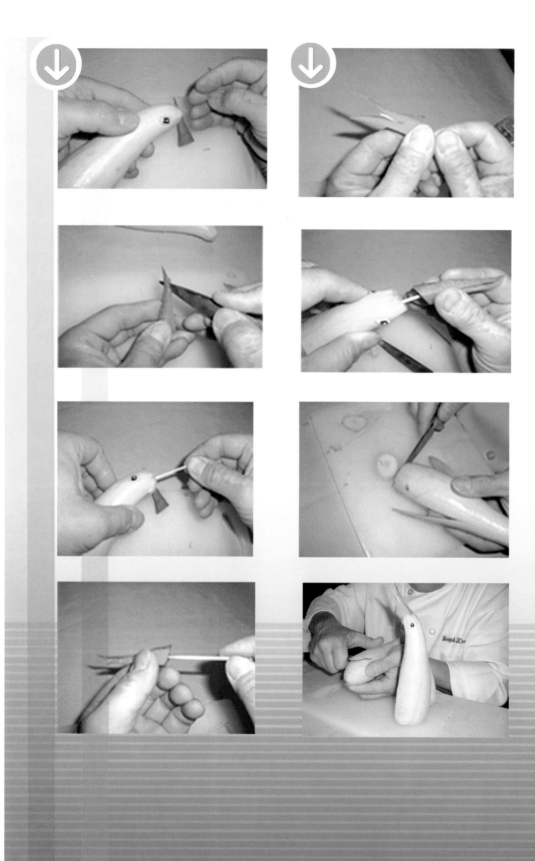

Honey, I always love you !

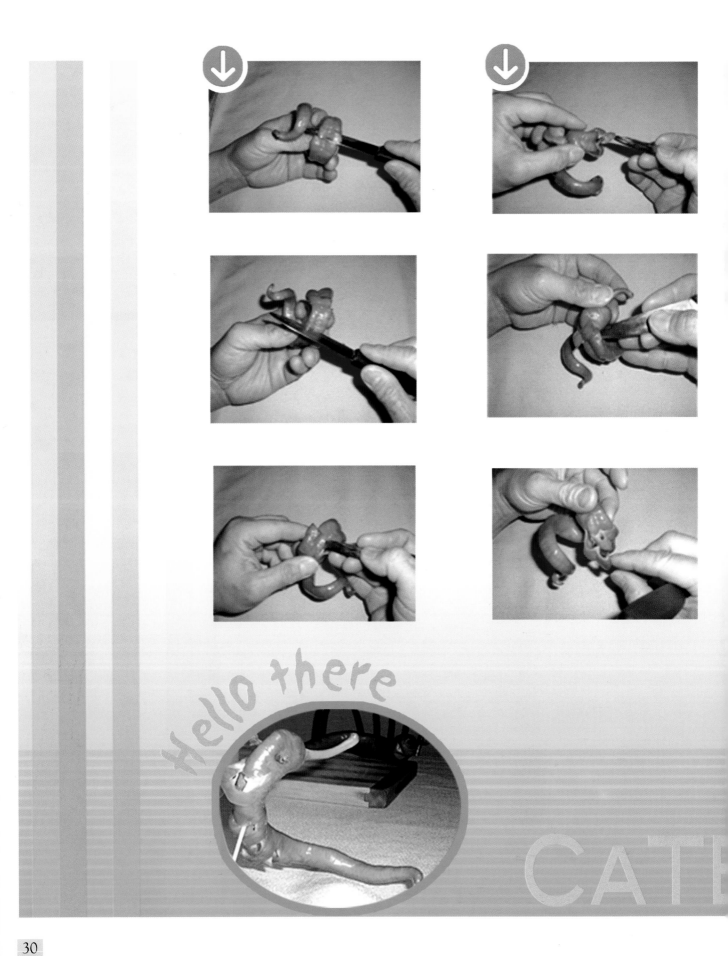

Hello there

Caterpillar (from a Hot Pepper)
Don't Let your Sculpture Make you Cry

This caterpillar is made from hot pepper. Wash your hands completely when you are done, or you might cry from hot pepper juice when you touch your eyes, or you might burn your butt if you go to bathroom. Good Luck!

RPILLAR

樂在其中

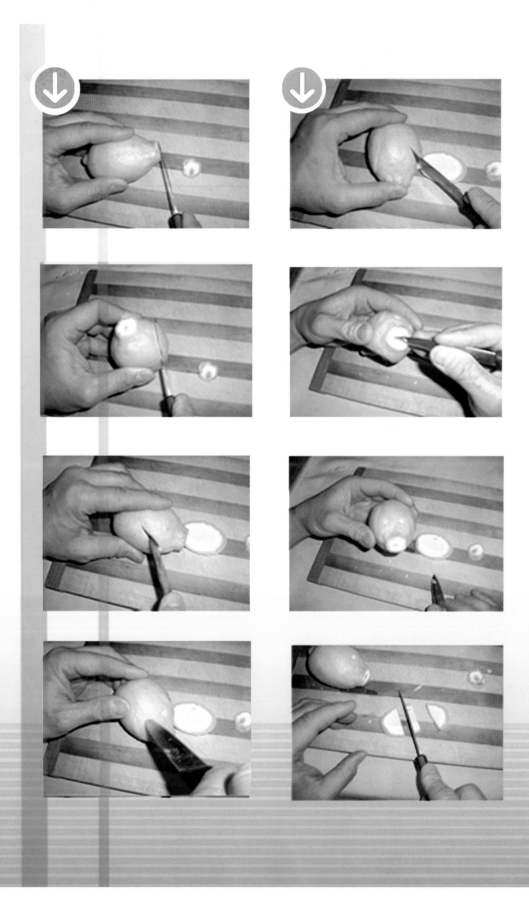

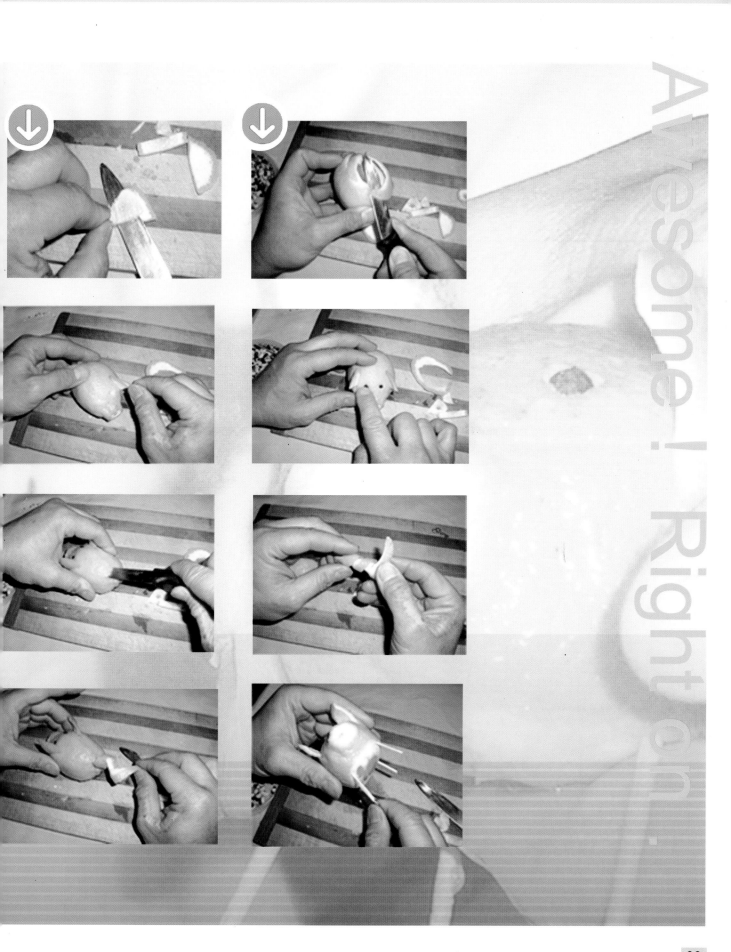

33

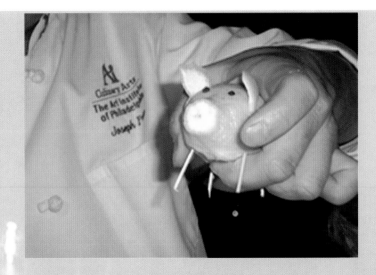

Lemon Pig: Don t Take Things from A Stranger!

I love to do demo of making a lemon pig to kids. I remember one time when I finished, I ask them, "Who wants this little piggy?" I heard many voices, "I do! I do! I do!" I walked to a naughty kid who really wanted this piggy. "Give me your hands please!" Then I told him, "Have your teachers and parents ever told you that do not take things from a stranger? Uncle Joe is a stranger!" I squeezed the lemon juice and "pee" on his hands. "See, you don't listen to your parents and teachers, this is a lesson. Next time maybe a big lesson, you maybe disappear and then hurt all the people who love you, if you don't listen."

This is only a joke to kids. But behind the joke is what I want to share with young people: don't be so greedy to take things that not belong to you, otherwise you'll get punished. I remember one of my employees stole my money and got fired. As American say "It goes around and comes around." Be honest! Be nice! People will treat you the same way.

Honesty and trust should be
basic human nature!

You been Naughty

...ove to share this with Philadelphia Culinary Art Institute and Philadelphia Restaurant School students!

Little Piggy "pee" on my chopping board!

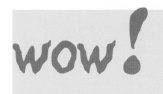 You think I create Asian Fusion Cuisine to "confuse" my consumers and students? Actually no!

Praise for Chef Poon's Cooking Classes

"Chef Poon class was fabulous. His warmth, brilliance and high energy make this experience a blend of theater, acrobatics and creativity. A master chef and a unique teacher, Chef Poon helped us make seven delicious dishes from one chicken." – A. Schwartz

"The class exceeded our expectations. Chef Poon was amazing. It was the perfect positive motivation to start the new school year. We will be back for more courses." – C. Rose-Meir, food service professional

"My son sent me to this class as a gift. He has always had a flair for great gifts, and this is one of his very best!" – P. Jucovy

You will discover new ways to cook. I will pass along a bit of culinary philosophy.

I want to share with you my secret techniques such as how to make seven dishes from one chicken.

I will show you my favorite recipes including five-second cooking, lobster magic, Peking duck and Asian fusion appetizers.

Chapter 3

New Ways to Cook

Asian Fusion Food and Joe's Recipes

1 pc Romaine Heart,
olive oil,
oyster sauce,
and Dijon mustard.

Pour a tbsp olive oil into boiling water.
Place Romaine Heart into boiling water for 5 seconds.
Put on the plate as the Romaine Heart is shining because of olive oil.
Add oyster sauce. Then add Dijon mustard. Enjoy it!

Five Second Cookin

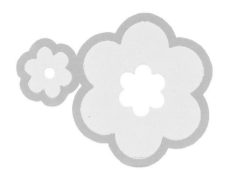

For a while, I ate in a restaura in Old City Philadelphia. Th had a recipe called Grilled Romaine. Romaine lettuce in the American supermarket costs up to $2.50 a bag. This restaurant used h the romaine and charged seven or eight dollars for the dish. The recip goes like this: Clean the lettuce, pu the lettuce on the grill until you see grill marks on the lettuce (this happens very quickly). Put the lettuce o the plate. Toss on oyster sauce, and Dijon mustard.

China mainland, Hong Kong and Southeast Asia have a similar recipe where we cook lettuce in five second Put the lettuce head in boiling wate with oil. Count five seconds, and li it out. The lettuce is still crispy. Dra the water and add oyster sauce. All done. This is my favorite dish in my life. I cook for customers all day, so it's nice to come home and have

I sprinkle some lobster roe!

something simple like this lettuce with a bowl of rice or noodles.

The philosophy of this recipe is using simple and inexpensive ingredients to make healthy, tasty food. By cooking the lettuce quickly, you don't kill the nutrients. If you cook lettuce too long, the fiber breaks down, and the nutrients wash away with the water. Then what you are eating is not as healthy. "The best dish is simple cooking and prepare!" says Auguste Escoffier, the father of French cooking. I saw these words in the library of Culinary Institute of America. This concept has great impact on my cooking philosophy.

Besides lettuce, you can cook other Asian vegetables quickly as well. Try bok choy or tender greens. If you have more than seconds, try Chinese broccoli, which takes only one minute and done! Remember, you don't need to add a lot of fancy sauce on the top. If you like, sauté some chicken, shrimp or scallops and place on the cooked Romaine Heart! You have protein to balance your diet.

These days, everyone is in a rush. You've heard of "One Minute Management." Now it's "One Second Management." Everyone moves fast, going here, running there. We have e-mail and cell phones to communicate in seconds. With so many obligations, we have less time to cook. But here, in only five seconds, you can complement a meal.

Simple Home Cooking!

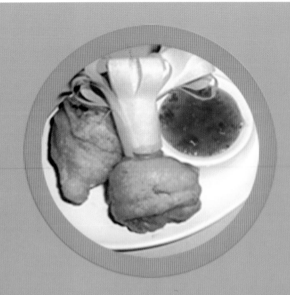

Fried Chicken Drum
(with Tangy Chili Thai Dip!)

General Joe's Chicken
(without flour!)

WOW! Make 7 dishes

This secret is "Mise En Place!"

**Ginger Chicken Soup
with Coriander**
(simple and healthy!)

**Honey Glazed Grilled Bourbon
Chicken Skewer**
(without bourbon!)

Stir-Fried Mango Chicken
(really healthy!)

Five Spicy Salt Chicken Wings
(stir-fry without oil!)

from 1 chicken !

Well prepare is half done! Yahoooo!

Ginger Scallion Chicken
(secret Chinese sauce!)

Thank you Diana for this cartoon! I love it. Does it look exactly like me?

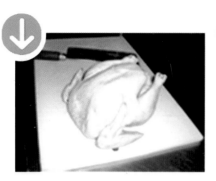

Smart cuts are the key.

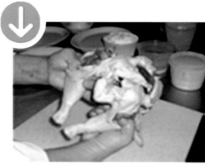

Break the legs.

How to Bone A Chicken in One Minute?
Follow step by st(
You are a genius.
You can do it !

One cut from the breast.

Cut the legs.

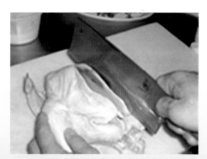

The other cut from the breast.

Start boning the breast.

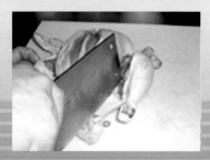

Two cuts from the leg.

Pull the breast.

Bone chicken filet.

Enjoy your cooking!

As I demonstrated on NBC Channel 10 and at ACF (American Culinary Federation). Yaah!

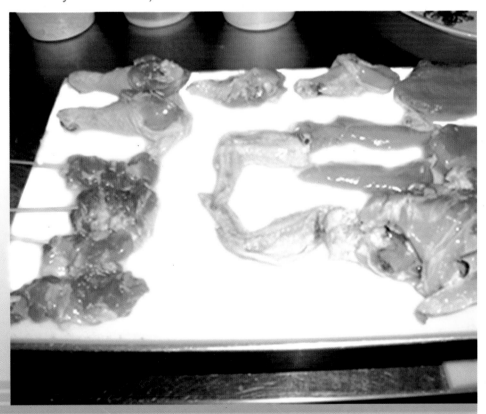

This secret is to concentrate and practice. "Practice makes perfect!"

Five Spicy Salt Chicken Wings

Ingredients:

1 lb. Chicken Wings

4 cups Soy Bean Oil for deep fry (low smoke point 410°F)

1 cup Dry Cornstarch

1/2 cup Sweet Red or Yellow Pepper, diced

1 tbsp Green Onion, diced

1 tbsp Shallot or Red Onion, diced

1 pc Long Hot Red or Green Pepper, sliced (option: Jalapeno)

1/4 tsp Five Spicy Salt (option: Kosher Salt)

Ingredients for Five Spicy Salt:

1 cup regular Salt or Kosher Salt

1/4 tsp 5 Spice Powder

5 Spice Powder: ground spices consist of equal parts of:

1. Cinnamon
2. Clove
3. Fennel Seed
4. Szechuan Peppercorns
5. Star Anise

Procedure:

1. Dust the wings with cornstarch.

2. Use very hot oil to deep fry chicken until it is cooked. (2 to 3 minutes, depending on wing's size)

3. Drain the chicken and set aside.

4. Heat the wok without oil, sweat all chopped ingredients and toast with cooked chicken wings. At the same time sprinkle with 1/4 tsp Five Spicy Salt.

Then Serve "Vol-Au-Vent" (Flying in the wind)

by Chef Joseph Poon
Joseph Poon Asian Fusion Restaurant

Yummy!

Sweet Red Green Pepper
Chopped Hot Pepper
Chopped Shallot
Five Spicy Salt

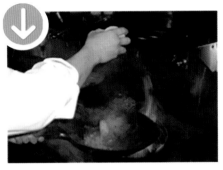

Sprinkle five spicy salt at the same time when toasting the wings.

"Vol-Au-Vent" (Flying in the wind)

Stir-fry the assorted pepper and shallot without any oil.

Me Funny Guy !

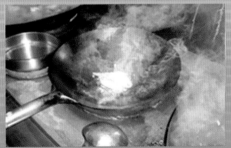

Place the chicken wings in.

Fried Chicken Drum

1 cup self-rising flour,
3/4 cup of water, mix them well; if
too thick, add a little more water; i
too thin, add a little bit self-rising
flour!
Be flexible! "Who moves my chees
Right?

Secrets to deep-fry:
Secret 1: Make sure the chicken
drum is 70% cooked in the boilin
water, otherwise when we deep-fry,
the batter will turn dark brown bu
the chicken meat is still raw inside

Secret 2: Either serve at once to ke
chicken wings crispy, or wait until
they become cool and soft, and de
fry one more time, which make ch
wings stand longer and crispy 5 to
minutes. That's what I learn "Dou
Deep Fry".

Sauce:
Go with Thai Sweet Chili Sauce, or
Chili Sweet and Sour Sauce, or
Blueberry Balsamic Reduction,
according to your flavor.

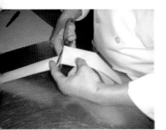

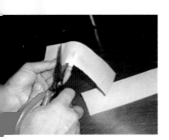

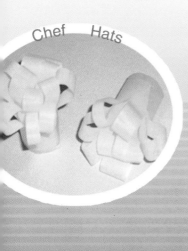

...e a chef hat for the chicken drum!

Chef Hats

Cut the skin completely off the bone.

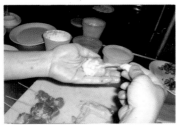

Then strip the skin all the way down to the other end.

Like this picture.

Dip into the self-rising flour.

The whole drum is covered with self-rising flour.

Holding for a few seconds before let go otherwise the drum will stick on the bottom of the deep fryer.

You can get this very tasty Thai Sauce in Asian Supermarket, about $2 a bottle.

Honey Glazed Grilled Bourbon Chicken Skewer
by Chef Joseph Poon
Joseph Poon Asian Fusion Restaurant

Use 6" bamboo skewers.

Oil the chicken before put on the grill.

Ingredients:

2pc Boneless Chicken Thigh

Marinated Sauce
1/2 c Light Soy Sauce
1/2 tsp Five Spice Powder
1c Water
1 tbsp Fresh Ginger Chopped

Honey Bourbon Glaze
2c Oyster Sauce
2c White Sugar
1c Sherry
1c Hot Water

Satay Sauce
1 tbsp Sah Cha Sauce
2 tbsp Satay Sauce
2 tbsp Coconut Milk
1 tbsp Evaporated Milk
2 tbsp Sugar
1 tsp Salt
1 tsp Curry Powder
1/2 c Ground Peanut

Procedure:

1. Cut boneless thigh into 3 long pieces.
2. Place into 1/2 cup Marinated Sauce for at least half an hour before using 6" bamboo stick to skew the chicken.
3. Cook the Bourbon Glaze until all the sugar dissolved completely, set it aside.
4. Grill the oiled Chicken, when it is almost done, brush the honey glaze on it.
5. Spray some Bourbon and sprinkle a spoonful chopped crunch roasted "Jimmy Carter" peanut.
6. Put the satay sauce on the side of the plate as dip.

Note:

1. You will need couple of 6" bamboo sticks and a brush for honey bourbon glaze.
2. This recipe can be used for BBQ Pork, beef and Salmon too!
3. Sauces can keep for one week.
4. Oil the chicken thigh to avoid sticking on the grill.

t is very tasty with "Jimmy Carter"!
He owns a peanut farm.)

As Chef Joseph Poon demonstrated on "The Ellen DeGeneres Show"

Marinate the chicken with water, salt and pepper.

Baking powder and cornstarch, for 10 minutes.

Dust with dry cornstarch.

Dust well and then deep-fry.

Deep-fry until golden brown and crispy.

Add oil, garlic chopped, hot pepper and ginger. Stir.

Add deep-fried chicken and sauce.

Thick the sauce by deduction or adding dissolved cornstarch.

General Joe Chicken
by Chef Joseph Poon
Joseph Poon Asian Fusion Restaurant

(2 servings)

Ingredients:

6 – 8 oz. chicken breast

1/2 cup dry cornstarch

General Joe Chicken Sauce:

1 tbsp White Vinegar

2 tbsp Light Soy Sauce

4 tbsp Chardonnay or any white wine

3 tbsp Sugar

5 tbsp Chicken Broth

1 tsp Chopped Garlic

1 tsp Chopped Ginger

1 tsp Hot Sauce

2 to 3 tbsp *Slurry

*Slurry: Thin paste of water and cornstarch stirred into hot preparation as a thickener!

Procedure:

1. Slice chicken breasts, marinate and dust with dry cornstarch.

2. Deep-fry chicken breast until brown. Place crispy chicken on the wok.

3. Add sauce and slurry. Then sir until all chicken is covered with sauce.

4. Place and serve with rice, decorated with crispy basil!

Excellent !

and Awesome !

Stir-Fried Fresh Mango with White
Meat Chicken

Marinate the chicken.

First blanch the chicken...

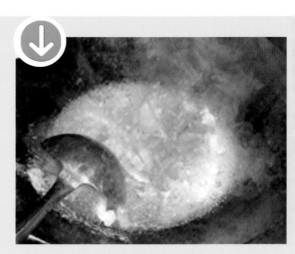

Add all the ingredients, for less than a minute. Then drain all the ingredients.

Assorted vegetables and fresh mango slice.

Into boiling water until 80% cooked.

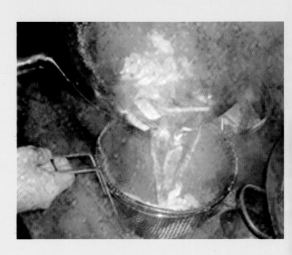

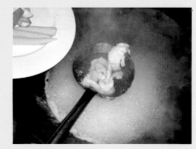

Enjoy Healthy Stir-Fry!

Stir-Fried Fresh Mango with White Meat Chicken

Chef Joseph Poon
Joseph Poon Asian Fusion Restaurant

Add oil, fresh chopped garlic and ginger.

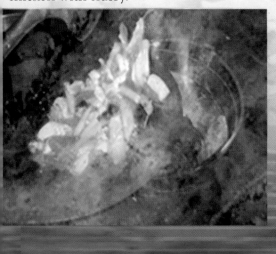

Then add blanched ingredients, and chicken with slurry.

Ingredients:

6 oz White Meat Chicken, sliced
4 pc Snow Pea
4 pc Celery (julienne cut)
4 pc Carrot (thin slice)
4 pc Yellow Squash (julienne cut)
4 pc Zucchini (julienne cut)
4 pc Mango Strip
4 pc Baby Corn

Marinated
1/4 c Chicken Broth
1/3 tsp Salt
A pinch White Pepper
1/2 tsp Corn Starch
1/4 tsp Baking Powder
1 tsp Sesame Oil
1 tbsp Vegetable Oil

White Sauce
1 tsp Fresh Garlic, chopped
1 tsp Fresh Ginger, chopped
1 tsp Shallot, chopped
1 tbsp Oil
1 c Chicken Broth
3 tbsp Cherry
1 tsp Salt
1 tbsp Sugar
1 tsp Sesame Oil

Procedure:

1. Very important to Marinate the chicken slice for at least 10 minutes before blanching in boiling water with all vegetable ingredients, because the chicken will become tenderer, smoother and tastier.

2. Add 1 tbsp soy bean oil in the wok, place all the chopped fresh garlic, ginger, shallot and vegetables. Stir and sweat all the ingredients before adding the white sauce with 1 to 1.5 tbsp dissolved corn starch.

3. Add a tsp of sesame oil at the last minute because you don't want to burn off the flavor of sesame oil as their smoke point is very low (410°F).

Boiling Water

Add chicken drum stick into boiling water.

Simmer for 30-35 minutes.

Put on the plate with ginger scallion sauce.

Ginger Scallion Chicken and

1. Ginger Scallion Chicken

Procedure: (very simple)
Put the chicken drum stick into boiling water. Then turn on low heat. Soak them about 30-35 minutes, depending on the size of drum stick. Then cut in pieces and use ginger scallion sauce as a dip.

Recipe for Ginger Scallion Essence:
1) 1 cup fine chopped fresh ginger without skin.
2) 1 piece of scallion, fine chopped.

3) 1/4 tsp of kosher salt or regular salt
4) 1 cup hot vegetable oil.

Mix all of them in a bowl and serve as A Dip!

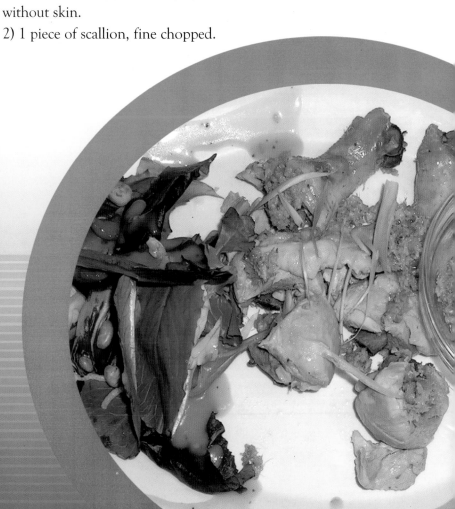

2. Ginger Chicken Consommé with Coriander:

Good for stomach with air, arthritis, and cold!

Procedure:
1. Put all the bones into a pot with 2-3 quarters water with a piece of fresh ginger.
2. Let it simmer (185°F) about 4-5 minutes.
3. Use a chinois and cheese cloth to drain the chicken broth.
4. Turn out a clear chicken consommé with a pinch (1/16 teaspoon) of salt, decorated with a piece of cilantro.

Awesome!

SOUP

Do you know how many different ways to name cilantro and scallion?
1. Cilantro-Chinese Parsley-Coriander
2. Scallion-Spring Onion-Green Onion

I like this soup very much. It is very simple, hot, healthy soup, same as mirepoix with fresh tomato!

1/2 Baked Lobster with
Hong Kong Secret
Mayo-Cheese

Lobster Appetizer: Crispy Angle
Hair Lobster Ball in Tangy
Chili Garlic Thai Dip

Lobster in Joe's Home Made
Moonshine Chili Tangy Garlic Essence
with Al Dente Linguini (Please don't
call 911 if it is too hot and sweet!)

Stuffed Lobster Claws Salad
with Jicama Swan

Lobster Magic:
Turn one lobster
into five dishes!

Surprise Lobster Mango Dessert?!

2004 year of monkey, "he" said
Don't worry, be happy, you have great future!

Joe, are you NUTS?!
Hey, this is 2005.
A lot of restaurants have
basil, wasabi or ginger
ice cream created by
chefs!

1/2 Baked Mayo-Cheese Fresh Lobster

I like the tender shanghai bok choy with a few drop of Lee Kam Kee oyster

Wow! Wow!

Magic Lobster ! Cool!

Baked Lobster:

1/2 Baked Lobster with Mayo-Cheese and Tender Shanghai Vegetables with Lee Kam Kee Simple Oyster Sauce

Procedure: (Go to next page for step-by-step pictures)

After the half lobster is cooked, take the skewer out.
Put about 1/2 cup Hong Kong Mayo-Cheese on the top of the lobster meat.
Then put into oven until the mayo-cheese turns golden brown.
Blanch some bok choy for side dish and put on Lee Kam Kee oyster sauce.

This is Hong Kong Baked Lobster and Shanghai bok choy served with Lee Kam Kee oyster sauce. Millions of Chinese restaurants in the world use Lee Kam Kee oyster sauce because it is one of the best simple seasoning ingredients! Highly recommended!

Hi !

Tips to pick lobster:

When you pick a lobster, squeeze the lobster head, if the shell is soft, put it back to the tank (but don't let the fisherman know, they will kill you); if it is hard, that means the lobster has firm meat. It is worth every penny.

Tips to cut a lobster and prepare cooking:

Cut claws and all legs first. Then cut the lobster into half, use one half to put in a 6" skewer and deep-fry at once before it turns watery. Cut the other half into 5-6 pieces, dust them with dry cornstarch, then deep-fry, and put aside after they are cooked, ready for another dish, Moonshine Lobster with Linguini.

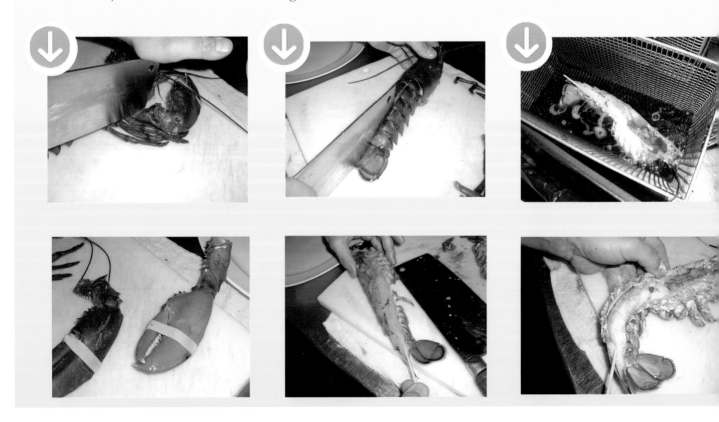

Charbroil the lobster.

Blanch the tender Shanghai bok choy in boiling water with oil.

Hong Kong Mayo-Cheese:
Commercial Chef Recipe

Place 1 package 16 oz 2% milk Kraft cheese with 2 oz butter, and a cup of chopped fresh garlic in a mixing bowl. Steam about 10-15 minutes until all the cheese melts. Then add one by one cup of Hellmann's Mayonnaise and stir constantly otherwise the Kraft cheese becomes lumpy, not smooth! Add about 10 cups of Mayonnaise but make sure the sauce still smooth.

This is one of the secret Hong Kong Recipes which I "stole" from one of the Hong Kong chefs! Shhhhh...Please don't tell anybody.

Crispy Angle Hair Lobster Ball
in Tangy Chili Garlic Thai Dip

It is not Cool !

It is sweet and crispy!

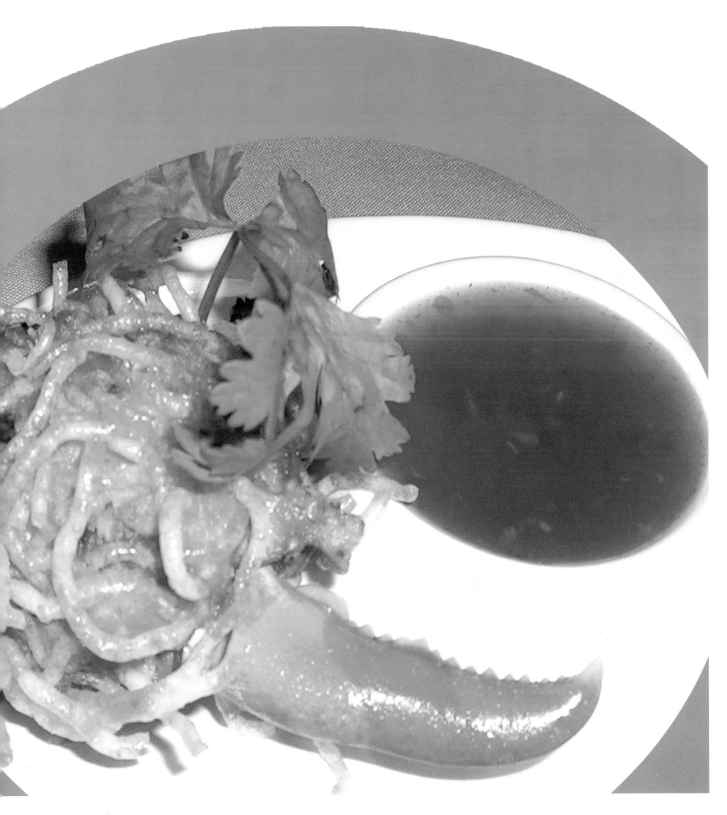

If you like to add basil or cilantro. It tastes better.

Water chestnut and shrimp paste.

Chop cilantro and ginger scallion.

Add chopped ginger scallion and cilantro.

Lobster Appetizer

Crispy Angle Hair Lobster Ball in Tangy Chili Garlic Thai Dip

This is stuffed lobster claws in ginger scallion water chestnut shrimp paste, served with Thai Sweet Chili Sauce.

Dust the lobster claw with cornstarch to help sticking with shrimp paste.

Dip into crispy rice noodle "angle hair", and shape it as quenelle.

Use a table spoon to make quenelle of shrimp paste.

Hold for a few seconds before drop into the oil so as to avoid sticking on the bottom of basket.

Note:

In some Chinese restaurants, it is served as Dim Sum. They use crab claws instead of lobster claws, usually $2 to $3 each piece!

Procedure:

1. Cut the claw into half.
2. Dust them with dry cornstarch.
3. Wrap them with ginger scallion water chestnut shrimp paste.
4. Deep-fry until they turn brown. Remember drop slowly into the oil to avoid sticking on the bottom of the basket!

Stuffed Lobster Claws Salad

This is stuffed lobster claws with mesclun salad, Wasabi Beans and healthy Roasted Soy Beans.

1. A piece of Jicama or apple to make a swan.
2. Dust the lobster claws with dry cornstarch.
3. Cover the claws with ginger scallion water chestnut shrimp paste.
4. Dust with dry cornstarch again.
5. Deep-fry for a minute until the claws turn golden brown and crispy!
6. Place in the center of the salad with jicama swan.

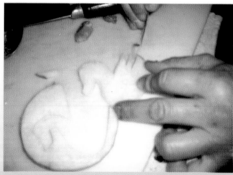

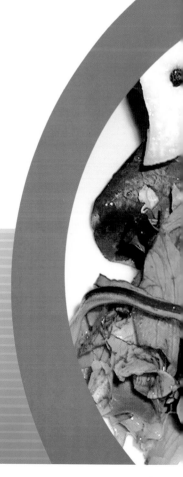

Look at the Beautiful
Swan !

Awesome!

1/2 Lobster in Moonshine Chili Tangy Garlic Essence with Al Dente Linguini

Hot! Spicy like my honey!

I make my Moonshine (sticky rice wine) in my kitchen. Please don't call "911"!

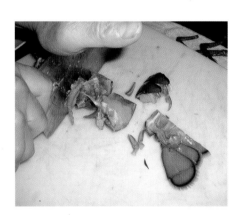

We make our own Sticky Rice Wine for this dish only. So I name this Moonshine Sauce.

Commercial Recipe for Moonshine Sauce:

3 1bs. Sugar

1 oz Salt

16 oz Fermented Sticky Rice Wine (from Chinese Grocery Store), option: Chardonnay

8 oz Fresh Ginger Puree

8 oz Fresh Garlic Puree

3 oz Hot Oil

1 can Catchup #10 Can

OOO !

nice

Procedure:

1. Blanch the cooked linguini for 30 seconds.
Don't over cook it, otherwise not al dente.
2. Place linguini on the plate.
3. Heat the moonshine sauce.
4. Mix with the cooked lobster pieces.
5. Use tong to arrange lobster pieces nicely on the top of al dente linguini.
6. Decorate with Pesto Sauce and a piece of cilantro.

Note:
Mama mia!
1. Do you know Italian cook noodles without rinse in water?
2. Do you know it must serve hot and al dente?

This Looks

Awesome !

Surprise !

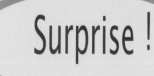

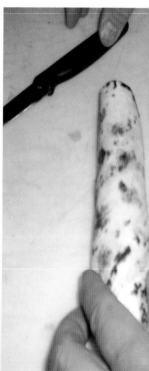

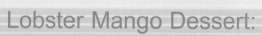

Lobster Mango Dessert:

Lobster Meat Mixed with Fresh Low Fat Mango Coulis, Fresh Mango and Jicama Wrapped in Grilled Tortilla or Phyllo Dough and Baked Decorated with Chocolate Year of the Monkey and More Mango Coulis

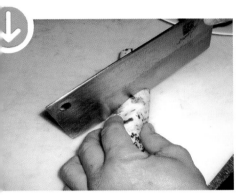

Procedure:

1. Cut the arms from the lobster claws and cook them in boiling water.
2. Then take the meat out, and place on the grilled tortilla.
3. Add mango and Jicama strips.
4. Mix with Mango Coulis.
5. Make a roll and cut in half.
6. Draw a monkey with chocolate syrup.
7. Decorate with more mango coulis and chocolate syrup.

Recipe for Mango Coulis:

2 cups diced fresh mango
1/2 cup low fat yogurt
1/2 cup confectioners' sugar
Put them into a blender, puree until smooth.

Year of Monkey 2004. Wish you all happy, healthy, and wealthy!

Peking Duck Taco

Peking Duck Tortilla

Peking Duck Polenta

Peking Duck
by Chef Joseph Poon
Joseph Poon Asian Fusion Restaurant

Ingredients:

One raw duck around 6 1bs. (You can get it from Chinese grocery store about $10.)

Peking Style Marinated
1 tbsp Salt

Sauce for Skin
2 gallon White Vinegar
1 1b. plastic jar Maltose (from Chinese Supermarket about $2)

Equipments needed
Large Pot of Boiling Water
Duck Hook
Large Fan
Place to Hang and Dry the Skin (at least 2-3 hours)

Procedure:

1. Blow the air to separate the fat and skin when you apply heat. The fat become more liquified and skin will become crispier afterwards.
2. Put 1 tbsp salt marinated inside the duck.
3. Put the duck in the boiling water for 15 seconds each side, then dip the entire duck in the sauce for skin at once.
4. Hook up the duck and hang it at a windy place until the skin dry then move to the high heat oven with a pot of water at the bottom of the oven to hold the dripping fat from the duck.
5. About 1.5 hours the skin will turn red brown and crispy.
6. Once it is done let it sit about 10 minutes and serve with pancake, scallion, cucumber and hoisin sauce.

The Secret of Making Peking Duck

Do you know Peking Duck not originate from Peking?

It originated from South of China— Canton and Hong Kong. In Qing Dynasty, a merchant went to the South to do business. He found Canton Roast Duck was very tasty. So he hired a chef from Canton to cook for him in his hometown, Nanjing. At that time, the emperor loved to taste the best food in different states. So the merchant pleased emperor with his loved Canton Roast Duck.

Then Peking Duck was first created and crafted to perfection by palace chefs. In 1911, court chefs who left the Forbidden City set up restaurants around Beijing and brought the Peking Duck to the masses. In 1976, President Nixon visited China and ate Peking Duck in Beijing. He loved it. Since then, Peking Duck has been popular in the United States.

Note:

If you use Chinese commercial roast duck oven over 800 thousands BTU, it takes only 55 minutes to roast 8-12 ducks, depending on the size of the oven and of ducks.
Don't over cook. Make sure the skin is dry before you put it into oven.

Do you know there is a big difference between preparing Peking Duck and preparing Cantonese Roasted Duck? Check my website http://www.josephpoon.com for details.

I created Peking Duck Tortilla in 1984 when I owned Joe's Peking Duck House! I created Peking Duck Taco and Peking Duck Polenta in 1997 when I opened Joseph Poon Asian Fusion Restaurant!

Peking Duck Tortilla

by Chef Joseph Poon

Joseph Poon Asian Fusion Restaurant

(8 servings)

Ingredients:

1 1b Shredded Duck Meat with Merlot Hoisin

1/2 1b Shredded Jicama

16 pcs Green Onion, julienne cut

8 pcs Grilled Tortillas 6"

Procedure:

1. Heat up the shredded duck meat with 1 cup Merlot Hoisin.

2. Grill the tortillas. Add shredded jicama and 2 pieces of julienne cut green onion.

3. Wrap the tortillas as egg roll.

4. Enjoy it!

Note:

Buy the Hong Kong Roasted Duck and bone the duck. Cut the meat in strip and stir-fried with 1 cup Merlot Hoisin sauce and 1/2 cup Red Merlot.

When you cook the duck meat, don't add any oil because we want to get more solid duck fat in liquid mixed with Hoisin and Red Merlot that will break down the fatty acid.

Hey, do you know I created this recipe in 1984 when I owned Joe's Peking Duck House. Now this dish is also very popular in my friends Tony Tang and Mr. Hung's Chung Hing Chinese Restaurant located at Cityline Avenue. I appreciate they help me to promote it.

Peking Duck Tortilla

Tortilla with healthy red caper salad.

Grilled Tortilla

Merlot Hoisin Sauce with wok seal duck meat.

Wrap and Roll.

Peking Duck Polenta

Ingredients:

Spring Mix Salad with Ginger Sesame Dressing or Balsamic Vinegar
Cooked Al Dente Linguini
Rosemary Polenta
1 cup Shredded Peking Duck Meat
1/2 tsp Sesame Seeds
1 pc Coriander

Procedure:

1. Grill the polenta.
2. Put two pieces on both sides of linguini.
3. Add more Hoisin Merlot Sauce on the top of polenta.
4. Place hot shredded Peking Duck meat on the top of linguini.
5. Sprinkle toasted black and white sesame seed on the top, and decorate with a piece of coriander.

Peking Duck Polenta

Peking Duck Taco

Ingredients and Procedure

1. Place 1/2 cup shredded lettuce and 2 tbsp diced tomato in a grilled 6" Tortilla.
2. Then place 1 cup of hot shredded Peking Duck meat with Hoisin Merlot.
3. Sprinkle toasted sesame seed on the top of the Duck meat.
4. Fold it as Taco Bell! Yeah!

I worked in Chili in 1995. I "stole" their ideas.
But I love to share with you.

Peking Duck Taco

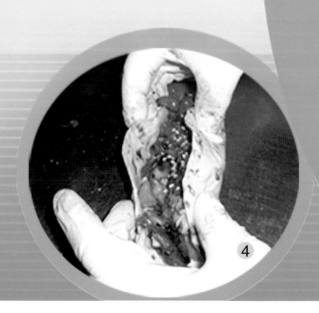

Indian Spicy Herb

Asiago Cheese

Yellow Banana Pepper Rings

Sun Dried Tomato

Five Spicy Salt

Asian Fusion Appetizer: Deep Fried Spinach
Fritti with Five Spicy Salt and Red Capers

by Chef Joseph Poon
Joseph Poon Asian Fusion Restaurant

Joe s Asian Fusion Appetizers

Ingredients:

1 bag dry clean Spinach
1 tbsp Asiago Cheese Powder
1 pinch (1/16 tsp) 5 Spicy Salt
1 tbsp Banana Yellow Pepper Rings and Sun Dried Tomato
1 pinch (1/16 tsp) Indian Spicy Herb (Cumin, Spicy, Garlic)
1 tbsp Scallion, diced
10 c Oil for Deep Fry
1/2 tsp Red Capers

Note:

For 5 Spicy Salt:
1/4 tsp 5 Spice Powder
1 cup of regular or Kosher salt

Procedure:

1. Deep-fry (350°F) the dry clean spinach about 1 minute until green leaves turn translucent. Drain all the oil.
2. Sprinkle the Five Spicy Salt and Indian Spicy Herb before adding Asiago cheese, red capers, chopped scallion and banana pepper rings.
3. Garnish with a piece of Chinese parsley.

Spinach Nachos!

Spinach Wonton Skin

Loose piece by piece before deep fry.

Cut into triangles.

Deep-fry the spinach wonton skin...

Until crispy.

How to loose the sticky Spinach Wonton Skin? Hold one end and hit the other end, then whole stack of wonton skin will be loose.

Note:
Parmesan cheese can be substituted for Asiago cheese.
You can get this green spinach won-ton skin in any Asian supermarket in USA, for example, West coast you can get from Winghing.com, ask Kenny Yee, President, and Matt Governanti, Director of Marketing. In East coast like Philadelphia, you can get it from Philadelphia Asian Supermarket.

Sprinkle mustard seed in duck sauce.

Asian Fusion Appetizer: Spinach Nachos with Asiago Cheese in Mustard Seed Duck Sauce

Ingredients:
1/2 bag crispy Spinach Nachos (Wanton Skin)
1 tsp Asiago Cheese Powder
1 pinch (1/16 tsp) Five Spicy Salt
1 tbsp Sun Dried Tomatoes
2 tbsp Red Green Pepper strips
1/2 tbsp Red Caper
1 tsp Scallion, diced
Dip:
1 cup Duck Sauce, 1/4 tsp Mustard Seed
Procedure:
1. Place the spinach nachos on the plate.
2. Sprinkle with Five Spicy Salt, Asiago or parmesan cheese,
sun dried tomatoes, red green pepper strips and diced scallion.
3. For dip, put duck sauce in small bowl. Sprinkle with mustard seeds.

Japanese Eggplant

Grilled Pita Bread

Sichuan Garlic Sauce

Red Caper Spring Mix Salad

Deep-fry to break down the fiber...

Keep the purple color bright and taste better.

Stuff the cooked Japanese eggplant in pita bread.

Do you know that Japanese purple eggplant has following characteristics?
1. Less acidity than Italian eggplant
2. Less fiber
3. Less seed
4. Good for digestive system
5. You can eat the skin too.

Diced purple eggplant

cut the pita bread in 6 pieces

Procedure:

1. Heat the oil in a wok. Add garlic, ginger and scallions. Stir constantly until the ingredients sweat. Then, sprinkle the merlot on the side of the wok.

2. Add diced deep-fried eggplant. Stir and cook about 1 to 2 minutes, depending upon the heat, until the eggplant starts to soften. Then remove from the heat at once, that's what we call "Carry over Heat" that I learned from CIA in 1977. Then, add 1 cup Sichuan Sauce to the eggplant mixture. Stir until the eggplant is covered with sauce.

3. Grill the pita bread and cut into 6 equal parts like a pizza. Stuff the cooked eggplant into the pocket of the pita. Serve hot.

Note:

Highly recommend whole wheat pita bread, because the white grilled pita will stick together and is harder to open.

Eggplant with Tangy Chili Garlic in Pita Bread

by Chef Joseph Poon

Joseph Poon Asian Fusion Restaurant

(2 servings)

Ingredients:

1 piece Japanese Eggplant, diced 1/8"

1 tbsp Soy bean oil

1 tbsp Fresh garlic, chopped

1 tsp Fresh ginger, chopped

1 tbsp Scallion, diced

3 tbsp Merlot, red

1 cup Tangy Chili Sichuan Sauce

1 pc Whole Wheat Pita Bread

Sauce:

1 tbsp Ground Bean Paste

3 tbsp Chinese Red Vinegar

4-5 tbsp Sugar

1 tsp Hot Sauce

2 tbsp Sesame Oil

1 tbsp Mushroom Soy Sauce

Pita Bread, grilled and cut into quarters.

I Love It !

Asian Potato Latke

by Chef Joseph Poon
Joseph Poon Asian Fusion Restaurant

Ingredients for large groups:

10 lbs. Potatoes, peeled, chopped, boiled then drained
1 qt.   Heavy cream
1 qt.   Italian seasoned bread crumbs
1/2 cup Fresh ginger, chopped
1 cup   Fresh cilantro, chopped
dash   Salt & Pepper
1 tbsp Butter

Ingredients for smaller groups

2.5 lbs. Potatoes
1/2 pint Heavy cream
2 cups   Italian seasoned bread crumbs
1/4 cup Fresh ginger, chopped
1/2 cup Fresh cilantro, chopped
dash   Salt & Pepper
1 tsp   Butter

Procedure

Dry all ingredients. Put all ingredients in mixer for approximate 2 minutes until well-mixed. If you feel mixture is still wet, add more bread crumbs. Let mixture sit in uncovered bowl on counter for 1/2 hour. Then make 3" ball and pan-fry it in Teflon pan (with no oil).

With C-CAP students, D'mark Rosseau and John G. Caucasian

I create this Asian Potato latke. Special thanks to Latkepalooza at The Gershman Y and Irene Levy Baker. They taught me Jewish culinary culture. Especially Irene sent me a traditional latke recipe. She encouraged me to create this Asian Potato Latke. Many people called me for this recipe after I helped latkepalooza fundraising. Now I share this recipe with you.

Another person I want to thank is C-CAP Carolyn Wimbush who sent two C-CAP students, D'mark Rosseau and John G. Caucasian to serve the latke and spicy salmon kebab during March of Dime event. I am happy to help C-CAP students improve their culinary skills and give them opportunities to get back to the community.

March of Dimes
Guy Przybycien Award
Winner in 2004 for commitment
to the community through
volunteerism and excellence
in the culinary arts

Questions and Answers

Who built Friendship Gate?

A: The Friendship Gate is located at Tenth and Arch Streets. This many colored arch ornamented with fire-breathing dragons and Oriental lettering was a joint project between Philadelphia and her Chinese sister city, Tianjin. Chinese artisans completed the Friendship Gate in 1984 with materials brought from Tianjin.

When was the first restaurant opened in Philadelphia Chinatown?

A: Most visitors come to Chinatown for its restaurants. People have been eating in Chinatown since the restaurant Mei-Hsian Lou opened in 1880. A plaque at 913 Race Street on the site of that first restaurant pays tribute to this eatery as well as the first Chinese immigrants who came to this country. America was known by those in China as "gim sa," or "gold mountain."

What was the first business in Philadelphia Chinatown?

A: In the 1870s, 913 Race Street also became the site of Lee Fong's laundry, the first Chinese business in the district.

What is the history of Philadelphia Chinatown?

A: Philadelphia's Chinatown is a compact neighborhood that does not approach the scale of the more famous Chinatowns in San Francisco or New York. Yet, the neighborhood's intimacy makes it especially attractive. Chinatown grew slowly until the 1940s and was considered a "bachelor society," peopled by mostly men. After World War II, a new wave of immigrants helped transform Chinatown into a family community.

Also transformed was the culinary front. The few early restaurants serv mostly Cantonese fare. Today one c get all manner of Chinese cuisine— Szechuan, Mandarin and Hunan. I addition to the dozens of Chinese restaurants, you can find several Vietnamese restaurants and a handful of Burmese, Japanese and Thai eateries located in Chinatown well. Vegetarians will find several restaurants catering particularly to their needs. But don't be surprised these vegetarian restaurants have "pork," "beef" or "poultry" on the menu—they're all made from high gluten, flour or a wheat product.

Praise for Chef Poon's Chinatown Tour

"What a spectacular tour! My husband and I felt as if we had uncovered a hidden treasure. Chef Po is truly amazing—a chef, an inventor, a dietician, an entertainer, and full of energy. He surprised us with gifts and samples along the tour. It was worth every penny." - A. Lee, Baltimore, MD

"I want to thank you for a fabulous tour. I go to Chinatown often, but now I feel like I've never real been there until today. What a great experience this was." - T. Novacich, Philadelphia, PA

"WOW!! What a truly fabulous, spectacular time we all had. The scouts ate every speck on their pla and really enjoyed the special places where Joe took us. We could have stayed with him for a few mo hours. He is one special soul." - C. Gosser, Troop Leader

"This tour might have been truly life-altering for my students. Most of them rarely meet people outs their culture and religion. And they rarely, if ever, venture to Center City, much less Chinatown. Parents said this was a once-in-a-lifetime experience." - L. Leff, Teacher, Souderton Charter Scho

Chapter 4

Philadelphia Chinatown Tour

Follow Me to Hidden Treasures

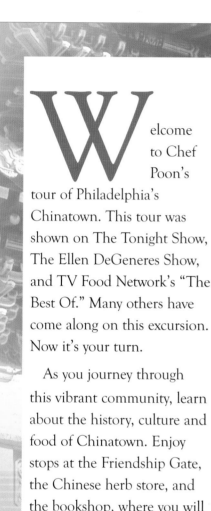

Welcome to Chef Poon's tour of Philadelphia's Chinatown. This tour was shown on The Tonight Show, The Ellen DeGeneres Show, and TV Food Network's "The Best Of." Many others have come along on this excursion. Now it's your turn.

As you journey through this vibrant community, learn about the history, culture and food of Chinatown. Enjoy stops at the Friendship Gate, the Chinese herb store, and the bookshop, where you will learn some Chinese calligraphy. Visit an Asian seafood and vegetable market. Step quietly through the Buddhist temple. Then watch with wonder and munch freely as you observe the inner workings of the fortune cookie factory. Now let's join Chef Poon.

The Friendship Gate

Good morning, America. Today we visit Chinatown. I call this my Wok 'N Walk tour. Sometimes I have 45 Girl Scouts join this journey through Chinatown, and other times only a couple of people. However many, I walk with them. I love to share our Chinatown culture. This place is unique and amazing. Some people pass through Chinatown everyday, yet don't really know this place. I have been here 33 years. I can tell you inside stories.

The first stop is Friendship Gate. America has many friendship gates, but this one is among the first ones built. Look at that—in the center of the arch are four Chinese characters. From right to left, the first one says, "Philadelphia." The second says, "City." The third says, "China." And the last one is what? Everybody guess. "Town!" Yes. Smart, you are!

You can see purple and red as background, with many gold dragons. A long time ago, in the Ming and Qing dynasty, no one was allowed to wear the gold dragon jacket except the emperor. Wearing this symbol meant you wanted to destroy the emperor. If you wore it, you and your family were killed right away. Now, who cares. Jackie Chan and Joseph Poon put on those gold dragon T-shirts anytime. Nobody kills them.

Many thanks to Philadelphia Chinatown Development Corporation along with its founders, staff and volunteers. They work hard to protect, preserve and promote Chinatown and Chinese culture.

Watch out when you cross the street. The Tenth and Arch Street intersection is one of the busiest areas in Philadelphia. Let's go to the next stop, Chinese herb store.

Chinese Herb Store

Here is the herb store. You can use these healing herbs in teas, soups and other food. This family business also offers acupuncture and herbal massages. The atmosphere in the store is peaceful. So when you enter, please keep your voices very soft.

Inside, you notice an intoxicating aroma. You feel a burst of awakening to the senses. This comes from the herbs set around the store.

Here you will meet the Chinese

I love to drink tea, especially green tea. Great to break down fatty acid!

herb doctor, an amazing man. He specializes in the ancient art of Chinese healing. This art has passed down though h family, generation to generation. These techniqu differ from those in Western culture. This healing art requires almost half a lifetime to master. The Chinese believe everything you eat is medicine and promotes healing.

The Chinese herb doctor can provide herbal remedies to help yo with colds, headache, upset stomac and so on. You tell the herb doctor

Saffron: Promotes blood circulation to remove blood stasis. Promotes menstruation and alleviates pain.

Pilose asiabell root (Dangshen): Invigorates the spleen, replenishes the middle-jiao energy, promotes the production of normal body fluids, and nourishes the blood.

Bupleurum root (Chaihu): Releases the exter and clear heat, pacifies the liver so as to relie stagnation, and elevates vital energy.

Cinnamon twigs (Guizhi): Promotes diaphoresis, relieves exterior syndrome, promotes blood circulation, warms the meridians and dispersescold.

Lotus Seed: Strengthens the spleen, relieves diarrhea, benefits the kidney to preserve essence, keeps the heart-fire and the kidney-water in balance, nourishes heart and tranquilizes the mind.

Honeysuckle: Clears hot, detoxifies, empties worries, makes eyes brighter, and promotes longevity and healthcare functions.

ur symptoms. He creates an exact
xture and writes down the herbs
u need. Then he gives you the
rbal mixture and the prescription.
is way, you can give the prescription
an herb doctor in a Chinese com-
unity anywhere in the world. That
ctor can then create the same
rbal mixture.

Here are some Chinese herbs and
w they can help you.

ote: Saffron

Do you know saffron is not only for
oking, but also great for blood circu-
ion and remove blood stasis?
Saffron is not always expensive.
Spain Saffron: $80-$100/oz
Chinese Saffron: $6/1b
Mexican Saffron Paste: $1.89/bottle

uctus Lycii (Joe calls "Red Caper"): Promotes
e production of essence, nourishes the liver,
ightens the eyes, and moistens the lungs.

stragalus Root (Beiqi): Invigorates vital energy
d spleen, strengthens the body, relieves skin
fection, promotes tissue regeneration, pro-
otes diuresis, and relieves edema.

I saw some sea horse and sea dragon on the top there!

Chinese Calligraphy

Come into the Chinese bookstore. Let me show you my favorite part—the Chinese calligraphy. For nearly two thousand years, the standards of excellence for this art have remained nearly unchanged.

When I was younger, we used an ink block and a bowl of water to practice Chinese calligraphy. We added water to the ink block to pick up the pigment on the brush. Then we stirred the brush in the water until the water grew black. Now you don't have to do that. You can simply buy a small container of ink at this Chinese bookstore for a dollar twenty-five.

To learn Chinese calligraphy, you can use a book that allows you to trace the characters. To practice, use a Chinese brush with a sharp point. The hair on the brush is very stiff at first. To soften it, wet it with water.

The size of the characters you're writing determines how much of the brush tip you need to wet. For small characters, wet only the tip. For large characters, wet the whole brush.

When you trace the characters from the book, use a light stroke. Don't press down too hard. And remember, in some Chinese calligraphy books, words are written and read up and down, from right to left. Each character stands for one word, unlike the English language where words are built from an alphabet of 26 letters. Chinese people have more than two thousand characters to learn. Some Chinese characters have more than one meaning, depending on where you place the characters.

You can learn Chinese calligraphy for free at my website, www.joseph-poon.com. You can continue practicing for as long as you like, because every month on the site, we offer a new character for you to work with. I really appreciate Nathan Salla who created this beautiful web page.

Trace & Learn
Chinese Calligraphy Set

This set includes:
• Wooden soft hair brush
• Ink box with cotton
• Small bottle of Chinese black ink
• A special book for the beginner to learn how to write Chinese calligraphy
  • A trace book which teaches you how to write each month

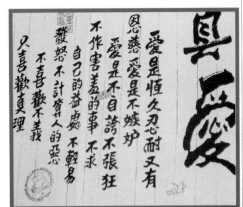

愛

愛是恆久忍耐又有
因為慈愛是不嫉妒
愛是不自誇不張狂
不作害羞的事不求
自己的益處不輕易
發怒不計算人的惡
不喜歡不義
只喜歡真理

良藥多苦口忠言多逆耳
淡中知真味常裡識英奇

Radish Mushroom: good for certain cancer!

This is not a holy communion. It is sliced dry abalone!

Asian grocery

Here we are at the Asian grocery. You can see display cases filled with alligator meat, oxtail, pork, beef, chicken and jellyfish. See the black Cornish hen? Guess what. When you skin this black hen, you find white meat inside.

Let me tell you about freshness. While giving lectures to executive chefs, I often ask them, "When you go to the seafood market, how do you determine if the fish is fresh?" Most chefs say things like this: If the eyes are not cloudy, the gills are not sticky, and the smell is not stinky, then the fish is fresh. In Asian culture and in Hong Kong where I am from, there's only one way to tell the freshness of fish: fresh fish is a swimming fish! We put the fish from the tank, kill it, scale it, skin it, filet it and cook it lightly in steamer!

Imagine fish on ice. Fishermen catch the fish out at sea. For one or two days, they keep their catch on ice in a box. The next day, they deliver the fish to the distributor. And one or two days after that, the fish arrive at the store for sale. These fish have been dead for four or five days. Swimming fish in tanks differ from fish on ice. Fish on ice have lost many nutrients

"A fresh fish is a swimming fish!"

Strip Bass in the tank

d natural flavor. Cells start to break
wn, and the vitamins begin moving
om the bodies into the ice. The
nger they stay on the ice, the more
ely this osmosis occurs.

In this seafood market, you do not see dead fish lying on ice. Instead you see large tanks filled with eel, lobster and crab. These tanks keep the catch alive to ensure freshness. Look at this fish. It's moving. It's fresh. When you

swimming fish, snappy crabs and squawking chickens. It takes these chefs less than five minutes to prepare the finest fish in the world. Once again you see, less time means healthy food.

un Dried Clam Meat

Sea Cucumber

Asia has almost a hundred different types of anchovies!

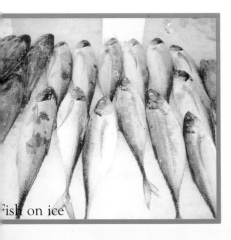

ish on ice

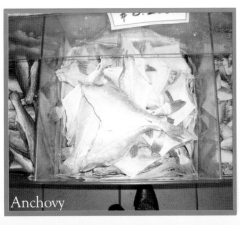

Anchovy

Fresh Oysters, Snails and Conches

More Anchovies

take these fish home, they are still alive. You kill them when you cook them. You find these same kinds of tanks if you visit other Chinatown grocery stores in San Francisco, Philadelphia or New York.

As you can see, Asian chefs love freshness. We want to make sure the fish is moving before we cook it. Most Asian chefs know a lot of skills to deal with fresh animals like

Freshness is tastier too. When you cook with fresh fish, you don't need much seasoning. Simply steam the fish with some ginger and scallion. Don't use a lot of sauce to cover the natural taste. And don't deep fry or panfry, because you will lose the nutrients, and all the oil will lead to greasy stuff. If you steam the fish fresh from these tanks, you will taste a fabulous, nutritional dish.

Asian nutrition concepts are completely different from American. Chinese think Food is medicine! Yin (cold) and Yang (heat) food must be balanced to keep healthy.

WARTER CHESTNUT 	Heals measles, aids urine, expels phlegm, and helps digestion.	It is extremely cold and laxative. Do not eat too much. Excessive consumption causes gas in stomach and abdominal swelling. Children eating too much might have severe pain under the navel. People with spleen and stomach asthenia should avoid. Pregnant women should avoid.
LOTUS ROOT 	Its juice is good for fever. Aids blood cells formation, stops bleeding and promotes urination.	Those with cold body constitution, spleen and stomach-asthenia or women before or after menstruation should avoid eating uncooked lotus roots. Cooked lotus roots, on the other hand, are warm-hot in nature. They stimulate muscle growth. Benefit the spleen, promote blood formation and stop diarrhea.
BAMBOO SHOOT 	Works as catalyst for small pox. Eat sparingly as they are hard to digest.	Excessive consumption would weaken Qi (vital energy). Those with spleen and stomach asthenia should not eat too often.
CHINESE CELERY 	Relieves fever, stops bleeding, and heals jaundice.	It is cold in nature. Those suffering from diarrhea, stomach and duodenum ulcer should not eat too often.
CHINESE CHIVES 	Various medical uses. Aids indigestion, expels phlegm and cures dysentery.	It should not be overcooked. Eating freshly can help to heal bruises. Cooked chive is warm and supplementing in nature. Those with abscess, wounds or eye problems should avoid. Excessive consumption causes dizziness. Do not eat with honey.
RADIS (white carrot)	Expels phlegm, and helps digestion. Cold in nature. Clears heat.	It is cold in nature. Patients suffering from debility, spleen and stomach-asthenia, duodenum ulcer, chronic gastritis or prolapsed uterus should avoid. It should not be eaten with warn-natured supplements in winter.

References:
Fung, S. N. (2003). Cook Easy! Eat Healthy! Fruit & Vegetables.
Hong Kong: Hoi Bun Publisher.

Fung, S. N. & Lee, W.S. (2003). Cook Easy! Eat Healthy!
Grains, Beans & Fungi. Hong Kong: Hoi Bun Publisher.

POTATO 	Do not have much medical use.	Excessive intake of solanine (produces from the buds of potato) might cause food poisoning symptoms like headache, abdominal pain, diarrhea, vomiting, pupil dilation and even confusion, paralysis of respiration and death. Pregnant women should avoid.
WINTER MELON 	Good for intestines. Acts as a diuretic. Reduces oedema and clears Heats.	Not recommended for asthenia-cold spleen and stomach, and thin body with weak Yin.
ANGLED LOOFAH 	Detoxifies and promotes blood circulation. Enhances lactation.	Not recommended for those who have digestion problems and diarrhea.
GINGER 	Expels the Coldness and warms the stomach. Stimulates hair growth and stops coughing.	Those with Yin-asthenia or accumulated Heat should avoid.

Asian Vegetable Market

Now come with me into the vegetable market. You can find many delicious ingredients. Over there, see bitter melon, ginger, lotus wood, water chestnut, seaweed, bamboo shoots, and amazing Chinese celery.

When I was a little kid, my parents often cooked celery for us. They made a simple, common soup of onion, carrot, celery, tomato, and pork or chicken bone. It sounds like French "Mirepoix"! All very simple, yet this is one of the most beautiful soup dishes in the world. Celery is mostly water and has high fiber, which helps decrease the risk of heart disease. Onion can lower blood pressure, lower cholesterol levels, and help prevent diabetes, infections and cancer. Carrot is full of vitamin C. This soup of simple ingredients is tasty and healthy.

In the same way Asian people prefer live seafood and fresh meats, we also choose fruits and vegetables in season. And we don't eat much deep fried food that can lead to overweight and high blood pressure. So for your health, instead of deep fry, try stir fry with vegetables in season. And try soup with lots of amazing vegetables as natual medicine!

Located at 6th Floor 1013 Race Street, Philadelphia

Pu Men Temple

(The Mystery of Buddhism)

When inside this temple, please step quietly. Walk to the left so you don't move onto the red carpet. If you take off your shoes, you can walk on the carpet.

Fortune Teller Paper

In the temple is a statue that some people say looks like Pope John Paul. The statue on the left is of a prince who kept the peace in the Tang Dynasty. Early in his life, this prince saw the suffering all around him after the war and wanted peace for his people. He walked to India to study Buddhism, and he returned to China to teach his people what he learned.

You can see a Buddha statue in the middle of this temple. Buddha is to Buddhists as Jesus is to Christians. Various kinds of Buddha statues represent different things. Be careful which Buddha belly you rub. For example, one Buddha statue holds a sack of money. If you rub his belly, you will have good luck with finances. Another Buddha has a small child with him. If you rub his belly ten times, mama mia, you will have ten children in one year!

While in the temple, usually take three incense sticks and light them. Then bring them with you to the front of the temple. Kneel in front of whichever Buddha statue you wish to

help you. While praying, hold the incense above your head towards the Buddha. The three incense sticks symbolize wishes for your beloved. When you finish praying, leave the incense burning in the pot in front of the Buddha. You will see a metal or wooden bowl with a stick lying beside it. As you finish each prayer, hit the bowl with the stick. In this temple, you will also find a fortune stick. This stick is filled with smaller sticks that have numbers on each one. Shack the large fortune stick until one of the smaller sticks falls out. Pick up the stick, and take it to a monk, here in the temple. Hand him the stick, and ask him a question. By looking at the stick, he will be able to answer your question.

And here is something good to know: On the fifteenth day of every month, according to Chinese calendar, this temple offers a huge free vegetarian feast.

This is a Good-Luck Buddha! Whatever you ask, you'll get it!

I think these kids must be hungry.
Let them try some healthy baked bun!

hinese Bakery

ome with me into the Chinese bakery. Notice the pastries and hot tea, similar what you might find in other keries around the world. Look ser, however, and you'll e some differences.

Unlike most American or European bakery items, these Chinese pastries are not fried; they are baked. This is another example of how the Chinese keep a healthy diet. The bakers do not load the pastries with sweet fillings or coat them with sugar. Instead they use pork, beef or poultry. These protein-filled treats are as affordable as the goodies you'll find at the donut shop. However, here for 55 cents, you can buy a much healthier treat.

What would a pastry shop be without cakes, pies and other sweets? You'll find these here, too. The difference is in the sweetness. Instead of using processed sugar, Chinese bakers sweeten their pastries with healthier choices such as fruit, fruit juice or raw sugar. The results are delectable.

One of the bakery's special treats is a beverage called bubble tea. This is a Chinese red tea with a European flavor. Instead of adding cream and sugar to the red tea as Americans do, the Chinese stir in black tapioca. They serve this bubble tea in a cup with a thick straw, so you can suck the tapioca into your mouth. This way of drinking tea originated in Taiwan. You must try this amazing beverage!

Note:
Do you know in Philadelphia Chinatown pastry shops are NOT the same!
K.C.'s Pastries—Hong Kong style pastry
St. Anna Pastries—Guang Zhou style pastry
Asian Pastries—Vietnam style pastry (Vietnamese Hoagie is great!)

Race and 9th Street, Philadelphia

Then the cookies go into a large bin where someone carries them to the packing machine. The cookies are individually wrapped and packed for shipping. The three machines make nine thousand cookies an hour! Let's take one. Hot, hot, hotter than my girlfriend! Don't open it yet because it is soft. I'll give everyone a bag of fortune cookies, since today is my birthday. Everyday I come here is my birthday! Yahhhh!

Thank you for coming along on our journey through Chinatown. I hope you all enjoyed the stories and many hidden treasures of this enchanting community. Good luck to you all in 2005!

To learn more about this tour, please visit my website at www.josephpoon.com.

Fortune Cookie Factory

Next stop—are you ready? This is the fortune cookie factory. This is an American thing, not something you'd find in China. Once inside, you will feel very warm. Look at this machine. It makes the cookie dough, which is similar to pancake batter.

Inside the machine, a hose pumps the dough and squirts it onto a turntable. These small pancake shapes pass through the oven quickly, so the dough stays soft. When the baked dough comes out of the oven, an attachment folds the cookies and, at the same time, inserts the fortune paper inside.

Joseph Poon

, who for 25 years helped elevate Philadelphia's restaurant scene, said he plans to close his landmark restaurant in Chinatown when his lease expires in October.

Poon, 56, said he will focus instead on his resaurtant consulting business and catering, but he is also considering starting a culinary school in Philadelphia to train chefs.

He is also widely known for his walking tours of Chinatown and for regular appearances on TV cooking shows, both of which he will continue.

"I don't think I would open another restaurant, unless it is part of a restaurant School," says Poon, who said his landlord's son plans to open a restaurant in the present location of Joseph Poon Asian Fusion Restaurant, at 1002 Arch St.

referenced from:
December 31, 2004 print edition
Poon cooks up eatery's end
Peter Van Allen
Staff Writer

Three-week Asian Culinary
Traveling Tour and Ten-day Asian
Culinary Secrets Training

- Total Fees:
$10,000,
- Traveling only
$6,000,
- Training only:
$4,000

Eating in China

- Beijing (3 day tour)
- Shanghai (3 day tour)
- Chengdu (3 day tour)
- Hongkong & Macao
(4 day tour)

Exploring Southeast Asian Food

- Singapore
- Malaysia & Thailand Tour

Ten-day Asian Culinary Secrets Training

(location: Philadelphia Joseph Poon Asian
Fusion Restaurant)

- Dim Sum
- Sushi Making
- The Secrets of Making Peking Duck
- The Secrets of Sauce
- Eastern Cooking Techniques and Ingredients
- Asian Kitchen Equipment

Two-week Asian Culinary Traveling
Tour Only

- Total Fees:
$4,500

More Customized Schedule...

Asian Culinary Traveling Tour
Why read thousands of books to experience
Asian cooking?

Experience the
Excitement in
Person!

If you are interested in this exciting culinary adventure with Joe Poon as your personal guide to the Asi
culture. Please fill out the contact form on the opposing page, and send it to:

- Joseph Poon/ Asian Adventure
- 1002 Arch Street
- Philadelphia, PA 19107.

You will be contacted ASAP when the form is received.
In addition to your becoming a part of this exciting adventure, you will be entered in the
"Joseph Poon Lucky Draw". This will give you a chance to win a trip to Hong Kong.

Joseph Poon Lucky Draw!

WIN A Ticket to Hong Kong!

or Cash $780

NAME	
PHONE NUMBER	
ADDRESS	
CITY / STATE / ZIP CODE	
EMAIL ADDRESS	

I would like to be a part of Joseph Poon Asian Culinary Traveling Tour.

Joseph Poon would love to know what you think. So please fill out the question below. THANK YOU!

Which part of the book do you like best?

What would you like to see included in a 2nd book?

What did you not like about the book?

Any additional comments about the book.

What do you think about Joe opening a traveling culinary school?

Published by Joseph Poon, Inc.
Philadelphia, PA
Copyright © 2005 by Joseph K.K. Poon

All rights reserved, including the right of reproduction in whole or in part in any form.
ISBN 0-9765596-0-9
Libary of Congress Control Number: 2005901538

Special thanks to my restaurant team!

When I spent my time writing this book, they helped me manage the daily operation of Joseph Poon As Fusion Restaurant, especially my head chef, Tony Qui, who has been working for me for ten years sinc 1985 at Joe's Peking Duck House, and Keung and Wah who has been working for me since 1997 I sta my Asian Fusion Restaurant.

The one I really appreciate is my manager, Jenny Li. She graduated from Drexel University, majored in Accounting. She works with my marketing agent Irene Baker to run my restaurant smoothly. Also she h me to deal with Wok'N Walk Tour of Philadelphia Chinatown, banquet, catering, cooking classes and m demos. Since she worked as full time, she helped me increase sale by 31% within six months.

Jenny Li and Irene Baker, thank you from the bottom of my heart!